THE HEBREW CHRISTIAN LIFE

Walking in the Way of Your Messiah

By:

Kenneth S. Albin

Kenneth S. Albin.
For more information about Kenneth S. Albin

www.savethenations.com
www.hitthemarktv.com

DESCRIPTIONS

WHAT ARE THE MOEDIM?

The Moedim are appointed days, rehearsals and special set times that God invites His people to gather as a congregation to meet with Him, their Creator and King. In God's sovereignty He has chosen, from the beginning of creation, seven appointed times during His calendar year.

WHAT IS THE SABBATH?

God has also, in His sovereignty, chosen another day that is set apart from the rest. God has pre-determined, by His sovereignty, to set apart the seventh day as the Sabbath for man to rest and to honor the Creator. The Sabbath was created for all of mankind, not just the Jew, Israel, but for all mankind.

WHAT DOES THE WORD FULFILLED MEAN?

A common misconception and misunderstanding of this word has caused much confusion. We tend to think of it as finished and that is why many Christians think when Jesus fulfilled something it means it is over and done, however in both the Hebrew and the Greek language it is does not have that meaning or understanding. Begin to think of this word in the terms of a marriage relationship where the vows are fulfilled not just one time or spoken on the wedding day but reconfirmed, upheld and strengthened throughout a lifetime in relationship. This is the correct understanding of the word fulfilled which is not a one time fulfillment but one with layers of fulfillments.

Fulfill is translated from the Hebrew word "Quwm" Strongs # 86965
To meet the requirement, to obey, to confirm, to establish, to prove, continue, strengthen and accomplish its goals, to make stand, to raise up, to continue or to perform.

Fulfill is also translated as the Greek Word: "Pleroo" Strong's #4137
"To fulfill, to complete, carry out to the full also well as to fill, bring to pass and ratify. The root of the word means there is nothing lacking.
The word is different from another Greek word meaning finished, completed or matured, which is the Greek Word Teleios.

WHAT IS A CHRISTIAN?

The word Christian is mentioned three times in the

New Testament. It is the Greek word Christianos. The term means "to be a little Christ" or "anointed". The term is used to point to a true disciple of Jesus Christ. A Christian is committed to following Jesus Christ, His teachings, His ways and His commands. The disciple of Christ will become more and more like Jesus as the Holy Spirit continues to work and conform their lives to the will of God. A real Christian has been born again and passed from death to life and darkness to the kingdom of Light. (Acts 11:26, Acts 26:28, 1 Peter 4:16, John 5:24, Colossians 1:13,)

WHO ARE THE JEWS?

The word Jew is a term used to describe those from the Southern Kingdom, tribe of Judah or the house of Judah. A Jew may also be from the tribe of Benjamin since that was the tribe given to David's descendants by the prophet Ahijah when he divided the two kingdoms and gave ten tribes to Jeroboam and two tribes to Solomon's son, Rehoboam. In the Southern Kingdom of Judah there were also some from the tribe of Levi and remnants of other tribes. These would also be known as being Jews or Jewish. The Northern Kingdom with ten tribes became commonly known as the house of Israel. God has given the Jewish people who came descended from father Abraham a mission to be a light to the Nations and to bring Messiah to the world.

WHAT IS A GENTILE?

The term Gentile comes from the Hebrew word Goy or its plural Goyim. It refers to the nations who were not physical descendants of Israel. A Gentile can also be used of the house of Israel, sometimes known as Ephraim, who lost their inheritance and identity when they, in their apostasy and divorce from Yahweh, were scattered to the nations, never to return. They are commonly referred to as the lost tribes of Israel. When a person accepts Jesus, he is "grafted-in" to Israel and becomes connected to and a descendant of Abraham by faith. It is important to understand that a Christian and follower of Jesus is no longer a Gentile. (2 Kings 17:23, Ephesians 2:11-19)

WHAT IS A HEBREW?

A Hebrew is the term meaning "one from beyond" or "crossed over one". It refers to Abram who crossed over the Euphrates River into a land that was promised by the God who revealed Himself as the true and living God. Abram crossed over spiritually to forsake his father's idols and worship El Shaddai.

WHAT IS A HEBREW CHRISTIAN?

Though the term is not common or usually connected, it should be. A Christian is a person who has crossed over from death to life and from darkness to light. This person is a disciple of Jesus Christ and follows His teachings.

A Hebrew Christian is a person who also embraces their inheritance and identity in connection to Abraham. The Hebrew Christian understands that they are not separated from, but connected to Israel, and receives the benefits of that rich tree and identity.

In no way is a Christian or a Hebrew Christian ever to think they replace natural Israel or the Jewish people. This is a dangerous and demonic doctrine that has caused many to horrors in the past. The Hebrew Christian is no longer hacked and no longer has their identity and inheritance stolen. They begin to see the Shalom of God working mightily "Nothing Missing, Nothing Broken, Nothing Lost, All Restored!"

WHAT IS THE TORAH?

Most commonly this refers to the first five books of the Bible known as the Pentateuch. The Torah can also refer to the entire Old Testament known as the Tanakh. Many think it means "law" or a book of "do's and don'ts", but this incorrect. The truest understanding of Torah is "instruction and teaching". The root word for Torah is yarah and it is an archery term meaning, "to hit the mark". It is composed of three Hebrew letters Yod-Resh and Hey. In the bible there are many synonymous words we can use for God's instructions including God's word, precepts, ordinances, ways, teachings, instructions and statutes. They are used interchangeably all throughout the bible. Yeshuah-Jesus and all his disciples would never teach anything that would cause a separation to the teachings that brought blessing and life to any one who would do them.

Throughout the Scriptures the promise of good things, life and well-being is connected and given to those who obey Torah. The New Testament word for sin Hamarthia in Greek means "to miss the mark". Also the Hebrew word for sin is Chattaah means also the same thing to miss the mark. It is so simple we most times don't see that sin causes us to miss the mark while the Torah instruction causes us to be in perfect alignment with God's Will, His Word and His Ways.

So when we obey Torah we "hit the mark" and live well, but when we sin by disobeying the Torah we get the consequences. The Torah, God's Voice and God's Word are all synonymous. (Deuteronomy 4:40, 5:29, Proverbs 6:23, Psalm 119:105)

TABLE OF CONTENTS

INTRODUCTION

I am so happy you chose to read this book because I believe you will be enlightened and encouraged as you reconfirm and strengthen your faith in the Lord Jesus. I want you to know that even though I was born Jewish I didn't understand what that meant or the mission God had for them. I did not understand the cultural context of the gospel after I got saved. My wife and I got married young and we learned powerful teaching in a church that taught and loved God's Word from Genesis to the maps LOL! We however were not aware of the deeper revelations of the scriptures that were hidden because of not understanding our identity as it related to Father Abraham. We also did not know that Satan himself who would consistently try to keep mankind from the blessing of the true tree of life by offering a counterfeit tree that ultimately will bring death. Satan had unleashed something demonic slowly but purposely. What he released was a spirit of division and separation that over time has brought a disconnection to the roots and ways of the faith.

This is what was sealed by the council of Nicea in 325 AD. Although man's intentions might have been good and noble because they did not know the true Hebrew Christian Life that was lived in the book of Acts and beyond they settled for a tree that promised what not only it couldn't bring but the exact opposite of what they should have been doing. Take a look at this text translated from the Greek language how they call the disconnecting from Passover or
Pesah as good news!

[1]We also send you the good news of the settlement concerning the holy pasch, namely that in answer to your prayers this question also has been resolved. All the brethren in the East who have hitherto followed the Jewish practice will henceforth observe the custom of the Romans and of yourselves and of all of us who from ancient times have kept Easter together with you.

Until the time of this council the church still kept the seventh day Sabbath and the Feast days that were instructed in the Torah. After this decree a death blow to all things that were considered "Jewish" and that would separate Christians from the culture of the leaders and people not just of Rome but the popular and accepted gods and culture of the nations.

[2] "Nicea, with its theological anti-Judaism, laid the groundwork for anti-Semitic legislation of later church councils. The Council of Antioch (341 CE) prohibited Christians from celebrating Passover with the Jews. The Council of Laodicea in the same century forbade Christians from observing the Jewish (and biblical) Sabbath. (Some Christians had been observing both Sunday and the Sabbath.) Christians were also forbidden from receiving gifts from Jews or matzoh (4) from Jewish festivals and "impieties." (5)"

I know this might be a lot of information but I want you to understand that for seventeen hundred years or more the ground has not only been laid but also now planted with crops that have multiplied the wrong fruit with the wrong tree, but we today accept it completely because it has become common and acceptable in Christendom. This book will help you discern biblically and see with a new lens so Christians can once again embrace their roots and true identity and bring the light and life of the gospel to the nations bringing them into the covenant and relationship that was first given to Abraham and now to all of His descendants though Messiah.

May the Lord open your heart and eyes to His Word and instructions and may you be about His kingdom business for such a time as this.

Sincerely,

Ken

CHAPTER ONE:

The Great Hack!

Recently I watched a commercial for a DNA test. The person who got the test results was now making a shocking discovery to a bloodline and a heritage that was previously hidden from them. The person emphatically stated how now they feel connected to whom they really are.

The blood in a person speaks to identity but also connects to destiny. The Great Hack has been deliberate and deceptive by the father of lies himself. He does not want you to know your true spiritual identity. He wants to keep the people who come to Jesus for salvation ignorant of what happens and begins at the time of conversion when a person is born again into a new spiritual identity and family.

The fact is that Christ has given you a spiritual blood transfusion and you now have the DNA of a descendant of Abraham. That means if it was promised to Abraham and his seed, it is promised to you regardless of your native born bloodline. This also means that you can trace your family tree back to Abraham. In your family tree you not only have Judah, but all the tribes of Israel. From Abraham came Isaac, then Jacob (Israel) and all his sons, both natural and adopted. You came from the seed of Abraham! If you believe in Jesus you can trace your physical family tree as Abraham's descendant. Most Christians don't ever fully realize this, but now it's up to you to embrace your roots, family lineage and the inheritance it gives you as a person who can trace his identity back to the one who crossed over into true worship, your father, Abraham. Those who begin to embrace the greater spiritual heritage and blessing found through our Messiah Yeshua-Jesus are now part of the exposing and debunking of the Great Hack.

Galatians 3:29 NIV If you belong to Christ, then you are Abraham's seed, and heirs according to the promise.

CHAPTER TWO:

Getting Back on Track

I can remember one day going with my daughter to the beach. When we arrived we placed our things on the sand and then we went down to the water and began to swim. We continued to have some time floating in the water quite unaware that the current began to cause us to drift away from the place where we had started. The place in the sand where we had our things was now not in our view. We had floated to a place that was no longer familiar and we had lost our bearings. This was not done purposely, for it just happened, as we coasted not really paying close attention to where our journey began. After a short panic of thinking our stuff was stolen, I realized that it was exactly where we left it. It was my daughter and I who had drifted away in the current. I can still remember thinking how easy it was to get off course.

Over a long period of time, most believers have

been unaware of a tide of water that has been carrying them away from the original design and intention of the Lord as well as the blessings that are inclusive to those who don't drift from the safety, protection and the life still available.

It will take a conscious effort for us to get back on track. This means the unlearning of some things that have been propagated and promoted as truth but is nothing more than man's attempt for wisdom without its true source. Reading of the bible by starting in the New Testament is like reading the end of the book before the beginning. You don't know who the characters are, the themes, the timelines, etc. It is like watching the sequel of a movie before seeing the prequel.

God's revelation for mankind began in the book of Genesis and to get on track you must start reading from the beginning.

Isaiah 46:10 Tree of Life Version (TLV)

10 declaring the end from the beginning, from ancient time, what is yet to come, saying, "My purpose will stand, and I will accomplish all that I please."

The Holy Scriptures will not make sense until you learn them from with a Hebrew Mindset. The entire bible has one seamless theme and the dots can be connected once you have the sometimes hidden key. Getting back on track means you have to get in the Bible for yourself and watch how that Word gets in you! Life will flow and the light of revelation will illuminate the path already planned from the beginning.

Proverbs 29:18 Complete Jewish Bible (CJB) 18 Without a prophetic vision, the people throw off all restraint; but he who keeps Torah is happy.

2 Timothy 3:16 The Passion Translation (TPT) [16] Every Scripture has been written by the Holy Spirit, the breath of God. It will empower you by its instruction and correction, giving you the strength to take the right direction and lead you deeper into the path of godliness.

CHAPTER THREE:

The Covenant

Today many modern societies are not as familiar with the concept of covenant. In ancient times it was understood that the covenant agreement was to be esteemed in the highest regard and because it was ratified in blood its terms and conditions would be followed even to following generations not even born. When God called Abraham from a natural bloodline filled with idolatry it was an invitation into a new covenant relationship. This meant the relationship would be bound by mutually accepted terms and conditions, but also rewards. This covenant was so strong and binding that today about 5000 years after that initial encounter it is just as valid and potent as it was when Abram (*His previous name*) was put to sleep and God walked in between the sacrifices and promised Abram with hope and a future to become a Father of Nations.

Genesis 17:1-9 Tree of Life Version (TLV)

17 When Abram was 99 years old, *Adonai* appeared to Abram, and He said to him, "I am *El Shaddai*. Continually walk before Me and you will be blameless. [2] My heart's desire is to make My covenant between Me and you, and then I will multiply you exceedingly much."[3] Abram fell on his face, and God spoke with him, saying, [4] "For My part, because My covenant is with you, you will be the father of a multitude of nations. [5] No longer will your name be Abram, but your name will be Abraham, because I make you the father of a multitude of nations. [6] Yes, I will make you exceedingly fruitful, and I will make you into nations, and kings will come forth from you. [7] Yes, I will establish My covenant between Me and you and your seed after you throughout their generations for an everlasting covenant, in order to be your God and your seed's God after you. [8] I will give to you and to your seed after you the land where you are an outsider—the whole land of Canaan —as an everlasting possession, and I will be their God." [9] God also said to Abraham, "As for you, My covenant you must keep, you and your seed after you throughout their generations.

This covenant blessing given to Abraham is now for all believers no matter the nation they were born or whatever natural heritage they have come from. The natural is not greater than the spiritual! In fact the scriptures are so clear that those who have been born from above have access to the same covenant and blessing as the native born seed of Abraham and Israel. Hallelujah! This means you have are no longer an outsider or stranger but family! You are now grafted into this covenant and get all its blessings, benefits and bounty!

The process of grafting has been done for thousands of years. In a sense it connects a foreigner or stranger to something that has a strong root and established foundation. Now, isn't this what the Bible teaches about those nations and foreigners who did not have a covenant, revelation or access to Yahweh, the living God, but now get the same because they are now connected to the root and foundation of Abraham through Christ?

God's plan was always to bring the Gentiles into covenant. This is the mystery of the gospel. I believe the scriptures are very clear on our identity when we are born again. God is not trying to make you Jewish, but remember you are married to Jesus from Judah. That is why I like to call myself a Hebrew Christian. I have "crossed over" from Egypt and the world systems into a covenant relationship with the one true God. Like Abraham, we are "crossed-over ones."

We have passed from darkness to light, from death to life, from sin to righteousness, from sickness to health, from poverty to blessing, and from brokenness into God's Peace. The Shalom that Jesus came to bring will leave us in a better place than before. His Shalom is "Nothing Missing, Nothing Broken, Nothing Lost, All Restored!" This is the blessing you are now blessed with!

Ephesians 2:12,19 Tree of Life Version (TLV)

[12] At that time you were separate from Messiah, excluded from the commonwealth of Israel and strangers to the covenants of promise, having no hope and without God in the world. 19 So then you are no longer strangers and foreigners, but you are fellow citizens with God's people and members of God's household.

CHAPTER FOUR:

The Hidden Gospel

It seems that the hidden gospel that the Apostle Paul and the disciples of Jesus preached from the beginning has been kept hidden from many believers today. In fact another gospel that could in fact be a tare has choked out and overtaken the genuine wheat of the true hidden gospel. Perhaps when Jesus spoke the parable of the wheat and tares it was pointing to a day like today. This watered down, powerless gospel is being proclaimed as the gospel of grace, but in reality it is nothing more than another bait and switch scam. It promotes and promises something quite contrary to the scriptures. It is one sided, unbalanced and insidiously drawing people away from the very life that Jesus and all the scriptures teach from the beginning. The gospel most people hear today is a mixture that is like a half-baked cake and a meal that has no whole food. Unfortunately the message of ultimate freedom has brought untold millions into bondage of deceit and lies because it is build on a foundation of sand rather than the rock of revelation of the Word.

The hidden gospel is one that connects every person through Yeshua-Jesus into a Way of Life! This true gospel has been cheapened into just a ticket to go to heaven. Heaven like other blessings are benefits of walking in the light of the covenant and a life of faith filled obedience by the power of the Holy Spirit. The gospel of salvation or heaven has been used as a motivator and hook to catch fish. The problem with that is the fish are jumping out of the boat as soon as they get in because they haven't been told the hidden and true gospel. In fact if you really examine closely the teachings of Jesus you will find as He teaches and the Torah instruction in a spiritual light it will seem more demanding than the commandments.

Matthew 5:19-22,27-28 Tree of Life Version (TLV)

19 Therefore, whoever breaks one of the least of these commandments, and teaches others the same, shall be called least in the kingdom of heaven. But whoever keeps and teaches them, this one shall be called great in the kingdom of heaven. 20 For I tell you that unless your righteousness exceeds that of the Pharisees and Torah scholars, you shall never enter the kingdom of heaven! 21 "You have heard it was said to those of old, 'You shall not murder and whoever commits murder shall be subject to judgment.' 22 But I tell you that everyone who is angry with his brother shall be subject to judgment. And whoever says to his brother, 'Raca' shall be subject to the council; and whoever says, 'You fool!' shall be subject to fiery Gehenna. 27 "You have heard that it was said, 'You shall not commit adultery.' 28 But I tell you that everyone who looks upon a woman to lust after her has already committed adultery with her in his heart.

So what is the hidden Gospel? It is the gospel that includes all nations into the same inheritance, same spiritual identity and same covenant that God gave to Abraham.

Colossians 1:26-27 NLT

This message was kept secret for centuries and generations past, but now it has been revealed to God's people. 27 For God wanted them to know that the riches and glory of Christ are for you Gentiles, too. And this is the secret: Christ lives in you. This gives you assurance of sharing his glory.

Galatians 3:7-9 New King James Version (NKJV)

7 Therefore know that only those who are of faith are sons of Abraham. 8 And the Scripture, foreseeing that God would justify the Gentiles by faith, preached the gospel to Abraham beforehand, saying, "In you all the nations shall be blessed." 9 So then those who are of faith are blessed with believing Abraham.

The Hidden Gospel was preached by God himself as the good news to all people almost the same words and the angels proclaimed at the Messiah's Birth! The gospel is so much more than going to heaven. It connects you to a people, a land, a way of life and a covenant!

Once you begin to get this understanding of the gospel you will see why you are now a get to person. You get to be grafted and included into a wonderful and rich identity and heritage. The roots are strong! The foundation is sure! The Way will become clearer in the journey. Don't separate yourself from the root and your identity for that is a trick of the enemy. The Hebrew Christian Life is not just a mindset; it is learning how to walk like Jesus did.

CHAPTER FIVE:

Grace is Not New!

A very common teaching today is dispensational-ist theology. It is a belief and way of interpreting the bible based on a view that God revealed Himself and deals with humanity in different ways and times throughout history. An example of this from that thinking is that before Jesus came was a dispensation of law and judgment, but since Messiah humanity is now in a dispensation of grace.

At first glance this seems to make sense. Because of this view or slant, some translations will have a bias against "law" and lean more towards the popular dispensationalist view on grace.

John 1:17 New King James Version (NKJV) 17 For the law was given through Moses, *but* grace and truth came through Jesus Christ.

This scripture about grace and truth coming by Jesus and Moses giving the law is not really contradictory but complementary once you realize the "*but*" has been added and is italicized. For it was not in the original text. There is no separation between the Law and Grace, in face they work together like two sides of the same one coin. Each side is unique and shows a different picture, perspective or story, but it is still one coin.

John 1:17 Tree of Life Version (TLV)
[17] *Torah* was given through Moses; grace and truth came through *Yeshua* the Messiah.

This version clears up the confusion and is much more accurate. Today we have been told that the Law is no longer valid or necessary, but is that what the bible really teaches?

Since we are talking about grace not being new, did you know that when Yawheh revealed His name to Moses that He told Moses that He was the God who is GRACE, GRACE! And MERCY, MERCY!

This is in Exodus 33 verse 19 and it is here Moses begs to see God's Glory and the Lord Himself Declares and Proclaims His name as two doubles back to back! When you see a double meaning two of the same words together in the Hebrew it gives an exponential emphasis to the readers as to the intent and meaning of that word.

In the Hebrew the Lord Himself declares that He is (Chanan, Chanan) (Racham, Racham).

Chanan is a word that means grace and favor and Racham points to God's mercy and love. There is no other way to look at the name; character of our God is full of favor and mercy!

The glory is God's majesty, His splendor and also His abundant supply! So how is this grace something knew if God said he is grace and mercy? I hope you are receiving this download and begin to study the scriptures without the bias of dispensational theology.

Malachi 3:6 Modern English Version (MEV) 6 For I am the Lord, I do not change; therefore you, O sons of Jacob, are not consumed.

So if God does not or has not or every will change, why do we believe that somehow in the Old Testament Scriptures before Jesus being a different God than in the New Testament?

A Big Fat Lie!

I hate to put it this way, but we have been lied to! When we let the scriptures interpret themselves and get back to the original language they were written we will see the once again seamless story and inherency of the Holy Scriptures in both Testaments always telling the same story about the one who walked and commune with man in the garden and will continue that quest forever.

The Lord has always been a God of grace, favor, mercy and love. The very meaning of the Hebrew word "Chanun" means to stoop down and to show kindness and favor to someone who is inferior! It means that God will answer petitions with His grace and favor!

The same God of the Old Testament who taught His people Israel to have love for the stranger, Is the same who sends His only begotten son to those on this planet greatly inferior and far from His Holy and perfect nature.

God stoops down with favor because He is and always will be Favor, Favor and Love, Love! Now that you know the truth about grace not being new, you will read the end of the book knowing the roots and foundation that gives the gospel so much more depth and meaning.

John 3:16 For God so loved the World (*stranger*)

Deuteronomy 10:19 New King James Version (NKJV) 19 Therefore love the stranger, for you were strangers in the land of Egypt.

Finally the book of Jonah is a book that demonstrates God's love for the Nations as the Lord directs a prophet from Judah to go to the Assyrian Capital city of Nineveh to a people who do not believe in Yahweh as their God and are absolutely not His covenant people. Yet in God's tender mercies and grace He will send a prophet to these same people who will one day come to swallow up and scatter the Northern House of Israel. How is that for Grace? Amazingly the Jews of today in the temple read the entire book of Jonah on the Day of Atonement Holy Feast day.

Jonah 4:1-2 New King James Version (NKJV)

4 But it displeased Jonah exceedingly, and he became angry. 2 So he prayed to the Lord, and said, "Ah, Lord, was not this what I said when I was still in my country? Therefore I fled previously to Tarshish; for I know that You are a gracious and merciful God, slow to anger and abundant in lovingkindness, One who relents from doing harm.

CHAPTER SIX:

Divine Appointments

One of the greatest mysteries of the bible are the Lord's Divine Appointed times called Moedim.

According to the book of Genesis, God has put His Moedim in place to mark religious festivals. These "divine appointments" are the right of the Creator and part of His sovereignty. We can argue from now until Jesus comes about this, but it won't change what God has written and revealed in His love letter to us about what He desires and expects.

The Moedim are given, not just to the Jew, but to all of mankind. Adam, Eve, Cain and Abel knew about them being given from the beginning. So when we talk about starting from the beginning we are talking about getting our lives in tune and synced to God's calendar. This means we need to find out what God's calendar is and the special set-apart days He wants us to observe.

By the way, once you get your true identity settled and know you are grafted in to the covenant that Abraham had and once you know you are connected to Israel and not replacing them, you won't be saying "Israel's" or "Jewish" feasts. You will now become scripturally literate in this area and see that they were always Yahweh's feasts that He, in His mercy and grace, has given us an invitation to participate in.

It will always take faith and corresponding obedience to access the blessings found in all of these divine appointments. The invitation that God has given us in these feasts come from His love and abounding grace that He gives to those who will humble themselves and position themselves to receive.

Genesis 1:14 GW
Then God said, "Let there be lights in the sky to separate the day from the night. They will be signs and will mark religious festivals, days, and years.

So from the beginning God put in His divine calendar His Moedim appointed days for His creation to meet with Him. They are "rehearsals" and remind us of what God has and will do. All of the Moedim are also prophetic and will signal and point to future events. Like prophecy, they will be confirmed and fulfilled in a fresh and new way as we celebrate them.

This is why it is so important to start learning about these special times and, by faith, start to keep them. This is a great starting point on your journey and learning how to "hit the mark". We cannot expect to hit the mark when we don't show up for our God-given appointments. He has made time for us and He expects us to respond to His goodness.

In the book of Leviticus we will begin to see seven appointments in a year. These are separate from the weekly Sabbath day, which is also special and set apart as the seventh day

Leviticus 23:4 NET
"'These are the Lord's appointed (*Moedim*) times, holy assemblies, which you must proclaim at their appointed time. (*Moedim*)

So what are the seven appointed days according to Leviticus? There are four of them in our spring season and three of them in our fall season in the United States.

SPRING FEASTS:

- Passover or Pesach
- Unleavened Bread or Chag HaMotzi
- First fruits of Barley HaBikkurim
- Pentecost or Shavuot

FALL FEASTS:

- Rosh Hashanah (also known as Feast of

Trumpets/Day of the Trumpet Blast or Yom Teruah)
- Day of Atonement or Yom Kippur
- Feast of Tabernacles or Sukkot

Each of these Feast have to do with present, past and future events. In a general sense the Spring Moedim can help us understand Jesus first coming to the earth, while the Fall Feasts can also point to the Lord's second return. These are just generalizations but remember that every Divine Appointment is set by the Lord Himself. It is easy to see and confirm by scripture how Yeshua-Jesus gave His life on Passover as the lamb of God, then was buried before the Sabbath of Unleavened Bread and then Rose on the third day corresponding to the First Fruit of the barley. We also know that the Holy Spirit came and filled the disciples at the end of the feast of weeks or Shavuot exactly on that special appointed day.

The Spring Feasts are easy for us to see because of we already know the scriptures for this. We however don't as easily recognize that the scriptures are filled with hints of the Fall Feasts in the New Testament but because we aren't aware of the customs, idioms and themes of those days they many times go unnoticed and obscured from our view.

Some of the words that correspond to the Fall Feast Days are awakening or awaken, sealed, day or hour, white, fine linen, trump, shout, remission, atonement, mercy, priest, cleansing and righteousness.

Because we most Christians today are not aware of what to us is hidden or subtle but to the audience of Jesus and the Apostles was very plain and clear. Sometimes because of our ignorance we have interpreted many scriptures and have come up with doctrines that would have never come to the mind of those who had been schooled in the Torah and the Ways of the Lord. I believe in these days many believers are being drawn supernaturally by the Holy Spirit into a new appreciation for all these things and embracing them as the Hebrew Christians they really are. Remember according to the scriptures if it happened to your people it happened to you. All the promises of God are yours because of Jesus our covenant connector. This is why I always say that you get to keep the Appointed Days but eventually you will say I want to and have to because these things are an integral part of how Jesus walked.

1 John 2:6 New King James Version (NKJV)
[6] He who says he abides in Him ought himself also to walk just as He walked.

P.S. If you want to know more, please get my books Hacked & Hit the Mark available on Amazon, they will fill in all the blanks and answer many of the hard questions people might have.

CHAPTER SEVEN:

Massive Misunderstandings

I know you might be thinking what is this guy talking about? I want to give you a heads up about some of the things that have kept people like you and me in the dark for a very long time. What I mean is the misinterpretations of scripture that are so common and familiar to us we don't even question its validity. You see it is a proven fact that if you hear a falsehood and lie long enough and loudly enough you will come to believe it as having been based in truth. So because most of us have heard things about God or His Word long enough and loudly we have come to take them as truth despite the errors. I want to deal with the following Massive Misunderstandings.

- We are no longer under the law but under grace

- Jesus fulfilled the Sabbath and Feast Days

so keeping them is not necessary.

- It is legalism to keep and obey the commandments the only thing required is love because love fulfills the law.

- Christ is the end of the law and it is no longer in play for the disciple and follower of Jesus

- The Jerusalem council made a separation between Gentile believers and the native Jewish ones. The gentiles only have four commands to obey!

I hope you get the idea! I can find many more, but if we deal with these briefly you will see that each one is a Massive Misunderstanding and twisting of the original intent and teaching of the scriptures that are consistent from the beginning of Genesis to revelation.

We are no longer under the law but under grace!

The confusion can easily be cleared up when you understand the context of the scriptures found specifically in Romans and Galatians. What the Apostle Paul really was teaching was the power of the kinsman redeemer to free from the curse of the law! The curse of the law came in the form of exile, the cutting off and the divorce and was specific to the House of Israel. The curse of the law was broken in in the Death, Burial and Resurrection and this was how God's wisdom was manifested in a way that would satisfy His justice, Mercy and Faithfulness as He promised to the House of Israel in the book of Hosea.

Galatians 3:13 New King James Version (NKJV)
13 Christ has redeemed us from the curse of the law, having become a curse for us (for it is written, "Cursed is everyone who hangs on a tree"),

When Jesus died He broke power of the law of divorce and separation that had kept the House of Israel from returning legally to their first husband Yahweh. The Torah Law that they were under would not allow them to come back to Yahweh who had betrothed them at Sinai on Pentecost.

Romans 7:1-3 Complete Jewish Bible (CJB) Surely you know, brothers — for I am speaking to those who understand Torah — that the Torah has authority over a person only so long as he lives? 2 For example, a married woman is bound by Torah to her husband while he is alive; but if the husband dies, she is released from the part of the Torah that deals with husbands. 3 Therefore, while the husband is alive, she will be called an adulteress if she marries another man; but if the husband dies, she is free from that part of the Torah; so that if she marries another man, she is not an adulteress.

The Torah law of divorce is only in applicable while a spouse is alive. When the spouse dies the widow can marry again. The Torah law would allow divorce, but not remarriage to the first husband. This is why Jesus had to die and free the House of Israel from their unfaithfulness and broken marriage vows. The resurrected Man will however will be eligible as a New Groom marry the bride who is also made new by the laying down of His life as an act of pure unselfish and redeeming love.

This is why both Ephesians chapter five and Romans chapter seven talks about a marriage of Christ and His Bride. He gave Himself for her!

Romans 7:4 J.B. Phillips New Testament (PHILLIPS)
4 There is, I think, a fair analogy here. The death of Christ on the cross had made you "dead" to the claims of the Law, and you are free to give yourselves in marriage, so to speak, to another, the one who was raised from the dead, that you may be productive for God.

Again to be clear the context of the scripture is a specific curse of the law and not the law or Torah in general.

Jesus fulfilled the Sabbath and Feast Days so keeping them is not necessary!

Another Massive Misunderstanding has to do with the word fulfilled and what it really means according to scripture. Growing up I thought fulfilled meant that it has been satisfied and completed. This is the most common way people even bible literate believers think fulfilled really means. Unfortunately this is not what the bible definition is.

We need to start thinking of the word fulfill not meaning of ending or completion, but as confirmation and evidence of something that is eternal and everlasting. Jesus is the fulfillment of the Sabbath rest, does that mean we don't celebrate the day God said to celebrate as an ordinance forever? Jesus fulfilled Isaiah 53 as the innocent lamb that was wounded, bruised and chastised and punished for us, does that mean we don't celebrate Passover anymore because Jesus fulfilled the Passover? Jesus is our Passover, but Paul teaches us to keep and celebrate the feast! ! He is our Sabbath Rest; He is the unleavened Bread & the first fruits of the many sons. This is good news and all a confirmation of what the Word of God by the mouth of His prophets all spoke about. The fulfillment of scripture doesn't end it but reveals it prophetically again and again.

When we talk about fulfilling we need to see Jesus fulfillment of scripture as the fullest expression or spiritual goal, but not a permanent ending. Another way to look at the word fulfilled is to fill up to the brim, to cram full, to execute, to ratify, to accomplish, to be obeyed, as it should be, It also means to carry out into effect or realization. So fulfillment will always bring strength and uphold and not end or do away with! This has been a Massive Misunderstanding that has caused doctrines and belief systems that aren't congruent with the revelation of scripture. This is what happens when we don't understand the Hebrew Christian Way that is cyclical and eternal in nature and not linear thinking.

A marriage vow is fulfilled not just one time but continually. Celebrating with anniversaries, faithfulness, intimacy, gifts, honor, trust, commitment does this many times over. It is fulfilled with serving one another or in sharing a meal together or even in sexual intercourse. Again the fulfillment is not a one-time completion but an extension and confirmation of the vows of marriage made on the wedding day. All these are fulfillments and bring strength and uphold the relationship. This is what also brings power and strength into your walk with God as you continue in the Word like Jesus taught!.

Matthew 5: 17-20 NKJV

[17] "Do not think that I came to destroy the Law or the Prophets. I did not come to destroy but to fulfill. [18] For assuredly, I say to you, till heaven and earth pass away, one jot or one tittle will by no means pass from the law till all is fulfilled. [19] Whoever therefore breaks one of the least of these commandments, and teaches men so, shall be called least in the kingdom of heaven; but whoever does and teaches *them*, he shall be called great in the kingdom of heaven. [20] For I say to you, that unless your righteousness exceeds *the righteousness* of the scribes and Pharisees, you will by no means enter the kingdom of heaven.

Colossians 2:16-17 WB

16 Therefore no man judge you in meat, or in drink, or in part of feast day, or of new moon, or of Sabbaths, 17 which be shadow of things to coming [which be shadow of things to come]; for the body is of Christ.

The Scripture should be read as "no one may judge you but the body of (Christ)." In other words, the world's culture and celebrations (holidays) are not to influence or make you feel you are wrong for keeping God's Torah and His special appointed days. This is just the opposite of what most people and translations point to. They tell you what I had been taught for years: "No one is to judge us for not keeping these days, for they aren't important anymore. They are just shadows and not the real thing, which is Christ. If you have Jesus, you no longer need these shadows!"

A shadow is the frame that is cast when the sun (light) is shining. A shadow is proof that something is really there. A shadow is not a negative, but a positive, for the appointed days of the Lord are to be celebrated now because they have a reality that is even greater in the future. If we are going to be celebrating them in the future then why wouldn't the church be keeping them now and receiving the revelation and blessing in them?

• *The New Moons, Feast days and the Sabbath are signs that confirm and point to a reality and a future.*

• *A shadow is only present when something of substance has light shined on it.*

• *The Moedim or Feast Days are prophetic signals that let mankind know that God has set times and plans for the people of the earth including the creation.*

The truth is that the feast days are not Jewish nor were they given to just the Jews. They were given back in the book of Genesis with the creation of the sun, moon and the stars. They were affirmed on Mount Sinai as Moses gave the Torah to all the tribes of Israel and the mixed multitude that were present. The feasts will be kept after the millennium and were kept by the New Testament church in the book of Acts and the Epistles. When the church synced its calendar with the world rather than the Jewish Christians the church became mixed with the culture of the world rather than the ways God had prescribed in His Torah instruction.

All flesh will one day be observing the Sabbath and appointed days. The scriptural evidence is over-whelming to keep them and not forsake them. Even Jesus in the Passover reminded the disciples to keep doing Passover in remembrance of Him.

Isaiah 66:22-23 AMP
22 "For just as the new heavens and the new earth which I make will remain and endure before Me," declares the Lord, "So your offspring and your name will remain and endure. 23 "And it shall be that from New Moon to New Moon And from Sabbath to Sabbath, All mankind will come to bow down and worship before Me," says the Lord.

It is legalism to keep and obey the commandments the only thing required is love because love fulfills the law.

Galatians 3:11-12CJB
11 Now it is evident that no one comes to be declared righteous by God through legalism, since "The person who is righteous will attain life by trusting and being faithful." 12 Furthermore, legalism is not based on trusting and being faithful, but on [a misuse of] the Be careful to obey all my com-

mands, so that all will go well with you and your children after you, because you will be doing what is good and pleasing to the
your God. text that says, "Anyone who does these things will attain life through them."

The key phrase is when we misuse the Torah commandments and say that when we keep them it brings us the righteousness that God accepts. The term legalism is now being used in a wrong way to depict anyone who seeks to obey God's ways. The keeping of them is not for salvation or to be saved, but it is an outward expression of our love for the Lord and the keeping of His commandments is a light that shines in a dark world.

Proverbs 6:23 NKJV
For the commandment is a lamp, And the law (Torah) a light; Reproofs of instruction are the way of life,

Romans 13:8-10 NKJV
8 Owe no one anything except to love one another, for he who loves another has fulfilled the law. 9 For the commandments, "You shall not commit adultery," "You shall not murder," "You shall not steal," "You shall not bear false witness," "You shall not covet," and if there is any other commandment, are all summed up in this saying, namely, "You shall love your neighbor as
yourself." 10 Love does no harm to a neighbor; there-

fore love is the fulfillment of the law.

Galatians 5:14 NKJV

14 For all the law is fulfilled in one word, even in this: "You shall love your neighbor as yourself."

The word fulfilled has been a word that has caused much confusion because we have been taught that fulfillment means, "it has been fully accomplished" or "now finished" or "complete". The word of God actually has promises that are fulfilled over and over as confirmations. So when we talk about fulfillment it can be fulfilled over and over with different people as well as in different generations and times throughout history. Every time we take the Passover elements of the wine and the bread we are fulfilling or confirming what Jesus did when He died for us.

So when you understand that love is the fulfillment of the Law, it doesn't mean that if you love you don't have to keep or follow any of the commandments. Love is the fulfilling of the Law because it will be love that compels you to obey God, which is the proof of love. Love fulfilling the Law means that when you truly walk in love you will obey what God has commanded.

John 14:19-26

[19] "A little while longer and the world will see Me no more, but you will see Me. Because I live, you will live also. [20] At that day you will know that I *am* in My

Father, and you in Me, and I in you. [21] He who has My commandments and keeps them, it is he who loves Me. And he who loves Me will be loved by My Father, and I will love him and manifest Myself to him." [22] Judas (not Iscariot) said to Him, "Lord, how is it that You will manifest Yourself to us, and not to the world?" [23] Jesus answered and said to him, "If anyone loves Me, he will keep My word; and My Father will love him, and We will come to him and make Our home with him. [24] He who does not love Me does not keep My words; and the word which you hear is not Mine but the Father's who sent Me. [25] "These things I have spoken to you while being present with you. [26] But the Helper, the Holy Spirit, whom the Father will send in My name, He will teach you all things, and bring to your remembrance all things that I said to you.

The Holy Spirit when He comes will be just like Jesus, He will continue to teach them, remind them and bring them in to the destiny and future like Jesus did.

Notice also in this passage Jesus talks about keeping the commandments, these are not exclusive commandments but the same commandments given by God from the very beginning. The keeping of the commandments were never a means to salvation but by our obedience to them it is evidence that we walk by faith and love. Love fulfilling the law does not mean you don't keep the law but the contrary. The proof of love is the keeping of the commandments. The commandments or the "Word" are God's love letter and invitation for us into a marriage covenant. The proof of love is that both parties in marriage honor are faithful in their hearts and actions. This fulfilling is not a one-time thing just like in natural marriage we fulfill our vows sometimes daily.

The word fulfilled has been a word that has caused much confusion because we have been taught that fulfillment means "it has been fully accomplished" or "now finished" or "complete". The word of God actually has promises that are fulfilled over and over as confirmations. So when we talk about fulfillment it can be fulfilled over and over with different people as well as in different generations and times throughout history. Every time we take the Passover elements of the wine and the bread we are fulfilling or confirming what Jesus did when He died for us.

So when you understand that love is the fulfillment of the Law, it doesn't mean that if you love you don't have to keep or follow any of the commandments. Love is the fulfilling of the Law because it will be love that compels you to obey God, which is the proof of love. Love fulfilling the Law means that when you truly walk in love you will obey what God has commanded.

So what did Jesus say about the proof of love? We tend to think that if love fulfilled all the Law then we don't need to do any of them. We don't need to keep the Sabbath days, we don't need to worry about not worshiping idols, for we just need to walk in love and if we do that we will be good to go. But is that what it means when we say all the Law is fulfilled in one word, love?

John 14:15 TLV
15 "If you love Me, you will keep My commandments.

John 14:21
21 He who has My commandments and keeps them, it is he who loves Me. And he who loves Me will be loved by My Father, and I will love him and manifest Myself to him."

Most Christians have been taught today that they no longer need to follow God's appointed days or the Sabbath. I like to teach that we are both Christians and Hebrews or Hebrew Christians who get to follow and keep what God had for all who are in covenant with Him. The Hebrew Christian understands that we can never replace Israel, but we are grafted and intertwined into the same root though Christ and the promise God gave to Abraham.

Christ is the end of the law and it is no longer in play for the disciple and follower of Jesus

Romans 10:4 ESV For Christ is the end of the law for righteousness to everyone who believes.

If we just take the Scripture at face value and not look at the Greek we will still get the same understanding. Christ is the end of the Law for righteousness and not the end of the Law like some people have interpreted. Just look at what Paul is preaching here.

The word end does not mean the Law is done away with, but actually means "the goal or the highest expression of why the Torah law was given." The word in the Greek is telos and means it is "set out for a goal or a definite point." So Christ is the "goal and point" of the Torah for righteousness.

We know that it was only Christ that could be worthy to die for our sins as a perfect Lamb and Man who kept the whole Law and did not sin in any way. Christ was the "goal of the Law for righteousness" as

2 Corinthians 5:21 New King James Version (NKJV) 21 For He made Him who knew no sin to be sin for us, that we might become the righteousness of God in Him.

The goal of the Law was for Christ to become our sin so we could
become and receive His righteousness. Christ didn't do away with the Torah Law. Paul would never say that. Jesus was the goal and He was the One all the Scriptures pointed to.

John 5:39 PT
39 "You are busy analyzing the Scriptures, frantically poring over them in hopes of gaining eternal life. Everything you read points to me,

> *The Jerusalem council made a separation between Gentile believers and the native Jewish ones. The gentiles only have four commands to obey!*

One of the most confusing passages that seems to separate the gentile believers from those born Jewish is Acts Chapter fifteen with the Jerusalem council dealing with the new gentile believers and how they are part of the called out congregation of the Lord known to us as the Church. Some may think that gentiles only have four laws to keep and they by the way are all part of the Torah Moses gave in the book of Leviticus. In reality they were a starting place for these believers who had no concept of the culture and thousands of years of heritage and covenant that was common to the majority of Jewish disciples. By the way even the four starting points given would have for sure kept the former gentile believers from eating unclean food another massive misunderstanding hidden in the idiom that prohibited the eating of things offered to idols. This was understood as to the eating of clean foods since the unclean foods like what would come from a pig was not even considered to be food for a native or converted proselyte to the God of Israel.

Since the Torah could not save anyone, the church leaders quickly agreed on these former Gentiles having their relationship with God
measured by anything but grace and faith. They give them four things to start with in their walk with God and remind them all that Moses' teaching is read and taught on Sabbath in the synagogue and they will learn as they go.

Acts 15:19-21 Tree of Life Version (TLV)

19 Therefore, I judge not to trouble those from among the Gentiles who are turning to God— 20 but

to write to them to abstain from the contamination of idols, and from sexual immorality, and from what is strangled, and from blood. 21 For Moses from ancient generations has had in every city those who proclaim him, since he is read in all the synagogues every Shabbat."

The former gentiles now believers would now attend synagogue services on Sabbath and learn the ways that Moses gave in the Torah. There was no separation; they were to be have One Lord, One Faith, One Baptism, One Torah and One Way of Life! As we read these same Scriptures again it is possible from this one story in the book of Acts that we would glean a separate system for those who are born Jewish and become Christians and those who come from the nations. If this were true then it would contradict a great deal of the Bible about the one flock, one Shepherd, one Church, one faith, one baptism, one Lord, one Father etc.

As these new believers get on God's calendar and growth plan by being in the House of God and learning God's ways they will eventually live by faith, the Holy Spirit and all that God has commanded for all believers.

Acts Chapter fifteen was a starting point, but God has promised to never leave us without finishing, for He is the Author and Finisher of all our faith.

Why would there be a separate "new way" for those

who were formerly Gentile believers and those who were born as Jewish believers? If this were the case then we should be able to search both Testaments and see the two different ways of following Christ. But you will not be able to find it because our God is a Father and a Good Shepherd who includes and brings into the family even sheep from another fold. He calls them all by His name and His own.

Numbers 15:13-16
13 All who are native-born shall do these things in this manner, in presenting an offering made by fire, a sweet aroma to
the Lord. 14 And if a stranger dwells with you, or whoever is among you throughout your generations, and would present an offering made by fire, a sweet aroma to the Lord, just as you do, so shall he do. 15 One ordinance shall be for you of the assembly and for the stranger who dwells with you, an ordinance forever throughout your generations; as you are, so shall the stranger be before the Lord. 16 One law and one custom shall be for you and for the stranger who dwells with you.' "

Isaiah 56:4-8 LB
4 For I say this to the eunuchs who keep my Sabbaths holy, who choose the things that please me and obey my laws: 5 I will give them—in my house, within my walls—a name far greater than the honor they would receive from having sons and daughters. For the name that I will give them is an everlasting

one; it will never disappear. 6 As for the Gentiles, the outsiders who join the people of the Lord and serve him and love his name, who are his servants and don't desecrate the Sabbath, and have accepted his covenant and promises, 7 I will bring them also to my holy mountain of Jerusalem and make them full of joy within my House of Prayer. I will accept their sacrifices and offerings, for my Temple shall be called "A House of Prayer for All People"! 8 For the Lord God who brings back the outcasts of Israel says: I will bring others, too, besides my people Israel.

CHAPTER EIGHT:

A Way of Life

I hope you are getting this message loud and clear. It is not my message or plan but the Lords! He has a way for all of us to live. It is the same way from the beginning. He wanted Adam His man to choose to eat of the tree of life. The choice was to live in the Way of the Lord or the way of man. It takes faith and trust to follow the Lord. The Way is found in God's instruction. It is How we Hit the Mark in life and also it is how we fulfill our Divine Assignments, Purpose and Mission for the life entrusted. So many people because they have not been taught the Torah Way have lived what I call a script for their lives that God never intended. God's Word is His Will! He will not change, does not or ever will change! He is not acquainted with dispensational or replacement theology. He has one way for His people to Walk it is the Hebrew Christian Life. Once you begin got walk out the Divine Calendar and commandments in His love letter you will stop trying to negotiate or bend the rules to fit into a self centered culture that has allowed its deadly thorns to poke and choke out the Holy Seed of the Word.

Psalm 19:7-11 CEV
7 The Law (Torah) of the Lord is perfect; it gives us new life. His teachings last forever, and they give wisdom to ordinary people. 8 The Lord's instruction is right; it makes our hearts glad. His commands shine brightly, and they give us light.9 Worshiping the Lord is sacred he will always be worshiped. All of his decisions are correct and fair. 10 They are worth more than the finest gold and are sweeter than honey from a honeycomb.11 By your teachings, Lord, I am warned; by obeying them, I am greatly rewarded.

God's ultimate intention is to be with us, in us and work through us. Every promise in Him is "yes and amen!" God is working in us to fulfill His good pleasure. If it is in the Word and it is good, then it is for you!
It is time to bring all of God's people into the unity and oneness Jesus prayed about. It is only when we follow Jesus and keep His commandments by faith that we are truly blessed. We must have a righteousness that is more than our confession and our words. We must have one that confirms that God's Word is alive and true!

I hope you will join me and the many that the Lord is drawing in these last days to walk as He walked and to embrace His ways and instructions. As you authentically embrace and walk in this Hebrew Crossed over life, this will be used to fulfill and confirm the prophecies about making Israel jealous and desire to know more about the Messiah that is for all mankind. A great revival and harvest will come and you are a part of it!

Romans 10:19 Living Bible (TLB)

19 And did they understand that God would give his salvation to others if they refused to take it ? Yes, for even back in the time of Moses, God had said that he would make his people jealous and try to wake them up by giving his salvation to the foolish heathen nations.

Deuteronomy 32:21 New Living Translation (NLT)

21 They have roused my jealousy by worshiping things that are not God;

they have provoked my anger with their useless idols. Now I will rouse their jealousy through people who are not even a people; I will provoke their anger through the foolish Gentiles.

As you begin to by faith and the power of the Holy Spirit walk in the Way of the Lord be aware that this will stir natural Israel back to their Father Abraham and it will also cause Christians who haven't been aware what has been hidden to search the scriptures and ask the Lord Himself to reveal what is true? I pray that you also keep the right attitude and posture to those who are ignorant and unaware and that you bring the light of the dawn with love and mercy to His beloved. Thank you so much for reading this book and I hope you have been blessed stirred and encouraged all for His Glory and Fame!

Numbers 6:22-27 The Message (MSG)
The Aaronic Blessing

22-23 God spoke to Moses: "Tell Aaron and his sons, This is how you are to bless the People of Israel. Say to them,

24 God bless you and keep you,

25 God smile on you and gift you,

26 God look you full in the face
    and make you prosper.

27 In so doing, they will place my name on the People of Israel—
I will confirm it by blessing them."

ABOUT THE AUTHOR

Kenneth was born in New York but as a young boy moved to Florida where he met his wife Lisa at her grandfather's church in Margate. They were married when Lisa was just eighteen years of age and at twenty-five she had their daughter Brittney. Presently Brittney has a beautiful daughter of her own with her husband A.J. her name is Brielle.

Ken founded Save the Nations Church with a handful of committed people who gathered in a home on September 17, 2006. Though God had put a vision in their hearts to reach the nations and bring light to a hurting world. Presently Ken and Lisa serve as the overseeing Pastors of the South Florida church campus meeting in Broward County.

After moving to Florida as a young seven years old Ken's parents were divorced shortly thereafter which left him deeply hurt for many years. During this time, Ken being Jewish went to Hebrew school and Temple regularly. At the time of his thirteenth birthday and Bar Mitzvah, many confirmed a calling as a "rabbi" or "cantor".

It was soon after this that Ken's grandparents met the Lord at a full Gospel businessmen's meeting. With momentum that came from above, Ken's Dad accepted the Lord as well as his mother who was is now serving the Lord full time in Messianic ministry with her new husband Rabbi Charles Kluge.

Ken being moved by his now "born again" Dad, was open to hear the message that his changed Dad's life. In the summer of Ken's sophomore year at Nova High school in Davie Florida, Ken met Jesus who radically altered his life as well.

Ken has been faithful to the house of God ever since then. He has served in Children's ministry, Youth, Worship, as well as in Associate and Senior Pastor roles for now over twenty years. Pastor Ken has an earned Bachelor of Theology from International Seminary and his Masters Degree from Liberty University. He is also an accomplished singer/songwriter who has written over 100 songs. He loves to worship with the guitar or the keyboard.

Ken has always preached the word with the inspiration and revelation of the Holy Spirit. He has been on a journey recently to bring Christians into an understanding of the roots of their faith. " The Christian church has been hacked!" as Ken states in one of his latest books about restoring the inheritance and identity back to the church.

As Founder of Save the Nations, he desires to inspire, instruct, resource and help people discover the destiny God has for them. The Nations has become their home as together they travel to the nations, teaching, reviving and sharing the resources that help make influential disciples and bring people into appreciation of God's Torah instructions.

Presently there two international Save the Nations churches in Rio and Marica', Brazil. Pastor Diego and Kelly are doing an amazing work for God and great fruit is seen in that nation.

Ken has authored many books and they are available on Amazon. They are being also translated to Spanish, Portuguese and Russian languages as well.

Ways you can connect with Kenneth Albin through social media.

BOOKS BY:

KENNETH S. ALBIN

YOU ARE BORN FOR THE EXTRAORDINARY

UPSIDE OF DOWN

THE MYSTERY OF THE CROWN

HACKED: THE HEBREW CHRISTIAN

THE PASSOVER BLESSING

NO MORE LEAVEN

HIT THE MARK

HIDDEN BLESSINGS REVEALED

TABERNACLES IT'S A CELEBRATION & NOT JUST AND OPTION!

HANUKKAH AND PURIM ARE FOR CHRISTIANS TOO

THE BLESSINGS OF PENTECOST

Contact Information for Ken & Lisa Albin
  www.savethenations.com   www.hitthemark-
tv.com
info@savethenations.com

---

[1]http://www.documentacatholicaom-
nia.eu/03d/03251965,_Concilia_Oecumenica,_Docu-
menta_Omnia,_EN.pdf
[2]http://www.yashanet.com/library/antisem.htm

www.ingramcontent.com/pod-product-compliance
Lightning Source LLC
Chambersburg PA
CBHW071636040426
42452CB00009B/1656